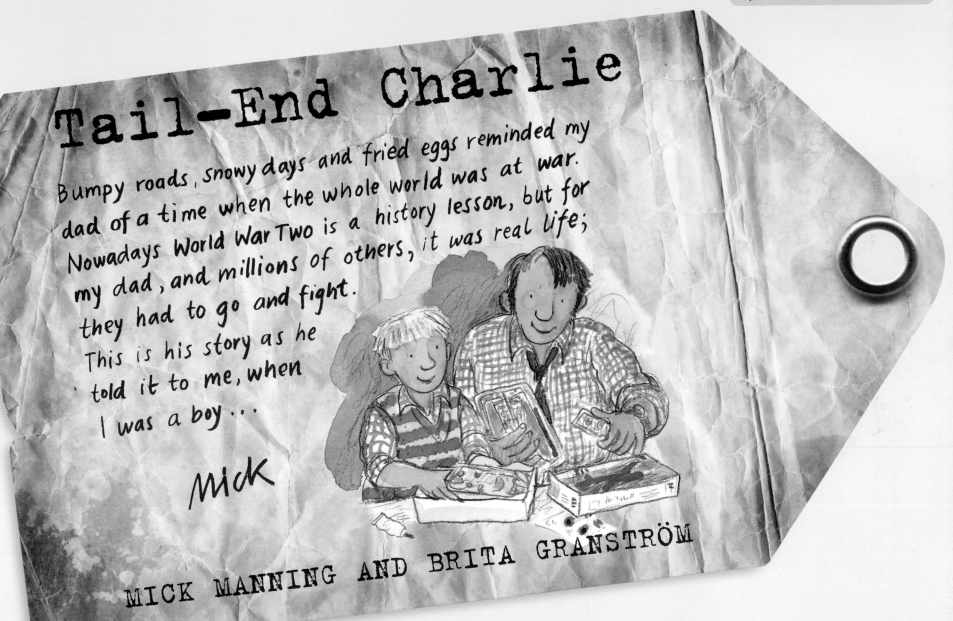

Tail-End Charlie

Bumpy roads, snowy days and fried eggs reminded my
dad of a time when the whole world was at war.
Nowadays World War Two is a history lesson, but for
my dad, and millions of others, it was real life;
they had to go and fight.
This is his story as he
told it to me, when
I was a boy...

Mick

MICK MANNING AND BRITA GRANSTRÖM

F
FRANCES LINCOLN
CHILDREN'S BOOKS

WAR BEGINS, 1939

Poached, fried, boiled or scrambled, I always loved eggs. But when I was a teenager World War Two broke out and fresh eggs were suddenly hard to come by. Shops only sold dried egg powder – ugh!

MUM MIXED THE EGG POWDER WITH WATER AND COOKED THE MESS – IT TASTED HORRIBLE!

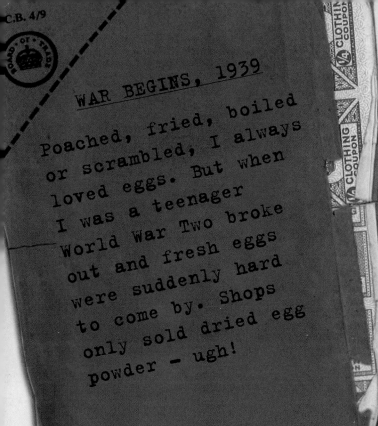

YOU NEEDED RATION COUPONS TO BUY MOST THINGS.

HOLD ON TIGHT!

I JOINED THE CIVIL DEFENCE, DELIVERING MESSAGES, PUTTING UP BARRAGE BALLOONS. SOMETIMES I'D BRING FRIENDS HOME FOR COCOA.

BOY'S OWN PAPER

6d

APRIL 194

LONDON SE1
8. 15 PM
28 NOV 194

2nd Tactical Air Force

Royal Air Force

Christmas 1944

This book is for Bill, Com, Paddy
and my dad, Charlie.
It's also for his grandchildren,
who never got to hear these stories:
Charlotte, Max, Björn,
Frej and Charlie Manning;
Tom, Emily and Alex Bland;
Dex, Flo and Amy Manning.

Tail-End Charlie copyright © Frances Lincoln Limited 2008
Text and illustrations copyright © Mick Manning and Brita Granström 2008
First published in Great Britain in 2008 and in the USA in 2009 by
Frances Lincoln Children's Books
4 Torriano Mews, Torriano Avenue
London NW5 2RZ
www.franceslincoln.com
All rights reserved.

ISBN: 978-1-84507-651-1

Printed in Singapore

1 3 5 7 9 8 6 4 2

Thanks to my father's comrades
for their patience, courtesy and
recollections: Dick Levy, Bill and
Huia Anderson, Ian Comrie, Jenkin William
Arthur Fowler and Malcolm Scott.
Also Russ Legross, 2nd TAF MBA archivist
staff at The RAF Museum and
The Imperial War Museum, London.

BOOK
PRODUCTION
WAR ECONOMY
STANDARD

THIS BOOK IS PRODUCED IN COMPLETE
CONFORMITY WITH THE AUTHORIZED
ECONOMY STANDARDS

Technical consultant:
F/O Richard Levy, Australian Pilot,
180 Squadron, 2nd TAF 1944-45.

RECRUITS, 1943

It was in "The Boy's Own" comic that I read about the RAF getting real fried eggs for breakfast. That made my mind up! As soon as I was old enough I enlisted to train as an airgunner. I was going to be one of Churchill's 'Brylcreem boys'.

ALL MEN OVER 18 WERE CALLED UP TO FIGHT HITLER'S NAZIS.

BUT FIRST I WAS TAUGHT:

ALWAYS SALUTE AN OFFICER!

PARADING AND SALUTING...

MARCHING...

28 O.T.U.

Date	Hour	Aircraft Type and No.	Pilot	Duty

After 'square-bashing' we were sent to 28 O.T.U., an Operational Training Unit, where we were assembled in a big aircraft hanger and told to pal up. I met three blokes looking for a tail-gunner: Bill, Com and Paddy. When they heard my name was Charlie, they grinned, because the nickname for a tail-gunner really was 'Tail-End Charlie'.

As a new crew, we got shooting, flying and navigation practice. Worst of all was 'ditching drill' – how to survive a crash-landing in the sea. We floundered around a cold swimming pool, in full kit, until we were exhausted. The instructor would duck us under before hauling us into the dinghy.

WE HAD TARGET PRACTICE IN A TURRET ON WHEELS!

EMV 957

ARE YOU LOOKING FOR A TAIL-GUNNER?

I'M A NAVIGATOR.

NIGHT OPs

AT THE BRIEFING WE'D BE SHOWN WEATHER REPORTS, MAPS AND PHOTOS OF OUR TARGET.

THE TARGET FOR TONIGHT, GENTLEMEN!

REMARKS	Unit	Cmdg. Officer's Signature

Our last training op was a real mission over enemy-occupied Holland to drop 'window'. These blackened foil strips confused German radar giving other RAF squadrons a chance to fly undetected by night fighters.

TAKE-OFF

Take-off was like the rattliest bus journey on the bumpiest road in the world. The noise was deafening, and when the bomber left the ground your stomach fell into your sheepskin boots!

WE CALLED THE FULL MOON A 'BOMBER'S MOON'.

	Flying Times	
Time carried forward:—		
REMARKS (including results of bombing, gunnery, exercises, etc.)	Day	Night

FROZEN CHOCOLATE

We scattered the 'window' bang
on target, high over Holland.
As we turned for home I relaxed
and opened my chocolate ration.
It was so cold up there that
the chocolate froze like a
brick. There I was, sucking
frozen chocolate, thinking that
the op had been a 'piece of
cake' when Bill, our skipper,
suddenly came on the intercom.
He said one engine had stopped
working! I peered out of my
turret. It felt lonely back
there with only the moon for
company....

TOTAL TIME ……

PIECE OF CAKE, SKIP!

THE 'WINDOW' WENT OUT IN BUNDLES TO
BE SCATTERED BY THE SLIPSTREAM.

YOU HAD TO SUCK THE FROZEN CHOCOLATE TO MELT IT.

Date	Hour	Aircraft Type and No.	Pilot	Duty

BANDIT

Then, in the moonlight, I spotted an enemy fighter following us! I muttered a warning to the crew and gripped the handles of my machine guns. I was expecting the worst. I'd heard fighters picked off the tail-gunner first. Sitting in my Plexiglas turret, I felt like a goldfish in a bowl, stalked by a black cat. He stayed on our tail as we limped home — but he never attacked us, and when we reached England he just flew away.

AFTER EVERY OP, CREWS GOT DEBRIEFED TOO.
ANY SCRAP OF INFORMATION MIGHT BE USEFUL.

IT WAS A WIZARD PRANG.

ONE ENGINE PACKED UP OVER THE NORTH SEA.

WE ONLY GOT HOME THANKS TO BILL.

EXPECT HEAVY FLAK HERE.

AT MELSBROEK, AIRGUNNERS GOT DETAILED BRIEFINGS.

BELGIUM, 1944

When we landed we found we were the only crew to complete the mission! Next day we were told we'd been selected for the 2nd Tactical Air Force. It was goodbye to night flying, we were re-trained to fly the B25 Mitchell.

We were posted overseas to join 180 Squadron stationed at Melsbroek. It's Brussels Airport now, but back then it was a war-torn Belgian airfield, just recaptured from the Germans.

THESE MITCHELLS ARE THE BEE'S KNEES!

I WATCHED THE GROUND CREW LOAD US UP WITH BOMBS.

BILL HAD HIS CAMERA AND WE POSED FOR A PHOTO.

TRIM? SET! MIXTURE? OK! PITCH? SET FINE! FUEL? TAPS FULL ON! FLAPS? LOWERED. GILLS CLOSED! GYROCOMPASS? SET. AUTOPILOT? OFF. GENERATORS? ON. SUPERCHARGERS? ON! OIL COOLERS? CLOSED. SEAT? LOCKED . . . READY FOR TAKE OFF!

BEFORE TAKE-OFF, THE SKIPPER CHECKED THE INSTRUMENTS. THIS WAS IT!

SOME SPITFIRES PROTECTED THE BOMBERS.
OTHERS FLEW HIGH OVER ENEMY TARGETS AND
TOOK PHOTOGRAPHS.

FIRST OP

Year	AIR TO GROUND Application % hits	Beam (day)		Beam (night)		AIR TO AIR—SLEEVE Quarter	
		% hits	% marks	% hits	% marks	% hits	% marks

Gazing out through the
waist-gun window, high above
Belgium, the fluffy clouds
looked like mashed potato.
Far below, the patterns of
autumn fields were like an
abstract painting or a
patchwork quilt.

It all seemed so peaceful.
But we were on our way to bomb
a bridge used by enemy troops;
we were going to try to kill
people and they were going to
try to kill us...

OTHER 2ND TAF AIRCRAFT INCLUDED THESE
TYPHOON 'TANK BUSTERS'.

WE FLEW IN A 'BOX' OF 6 AIRCRAFT. EACH HAD A DIFFERENT CODE LETTER LIKE S FOR SUGAR OR N FOR NUTS. 'EV' WAS 180'S IDENTIFICATION MARKINGS.

FLAK

Year	Individual (Day)	Individual (Night)	AVERAGE ERROR IN YARDS AS AT	
			Flt. (as leading B.A.)	Sqn (as leading B.A.)

As we approached the target, enemy anti-aircraft guns fired up a barrage of flak. It looked like cotton wool from a distance; black candyfloss. Flying into it, we found a nightmare of explosions and filthy smoke that stank of rotten eggs. Our plane shook with every blast and chunks of shrapnel whizzed through the sky. We watched in horror as other planes got hit and went down in flames.

ONE MITCHELL EXPLODED IN A BLINDING FLASH.

ANOTHER HAD A WING BLOWN OFF AND SPIRALLED LIKE A SYCAMORE SEED.

HOW DID WE EVER RELAX?

THE NAAFI SUPPLIED HOT DRINKS AND SANDWICHES.

WE LIVED IN AN OLD CONVENT. PADDY AND I PLAYED IN THE 180-SQUADRON SOCCER TEAM.

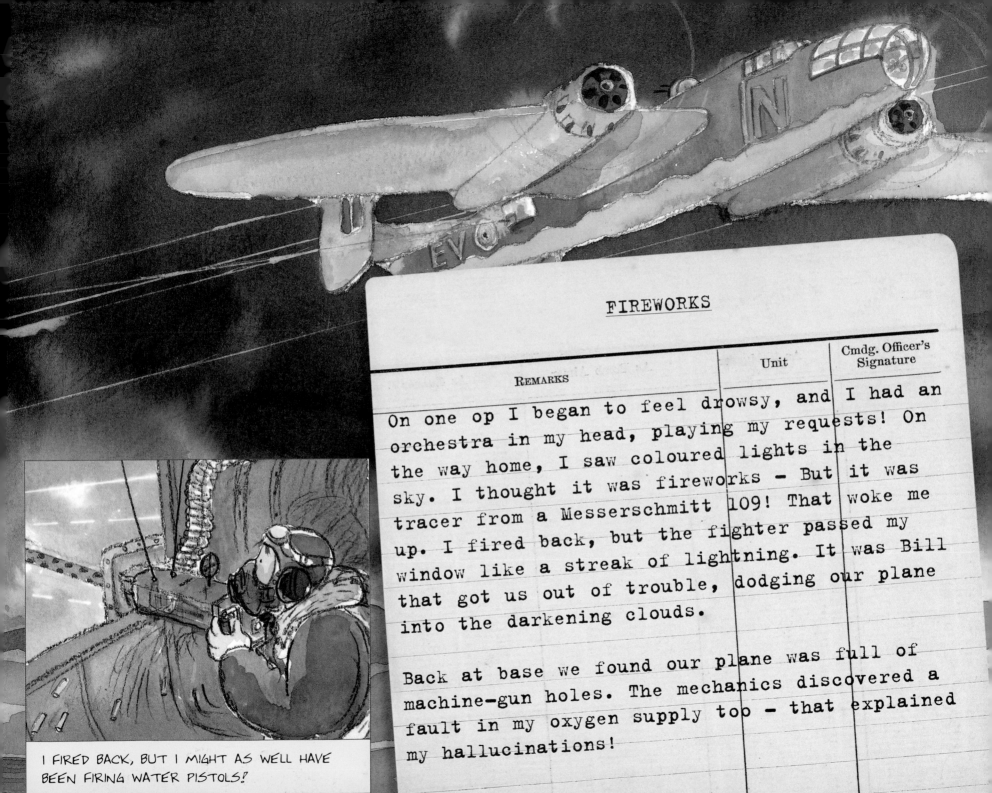

I FIRED BACK, BUT I MIGHT AS WELL HAVE BEEN FIRING WATER PISTOLS!

FIREWORKS

REMARKS	Unit	Cmdg. Officer's Signature

On one op I began to feel drowsy, and I had an orchestra in my head, playing my requests! On the way home, I saw coloured lights in the sky. I thought it was fireworks – But it was tracer from a Messerschmitt 109! That woke me up. I fired back, but the fighter passed my window like a streak of lightning. It was Bill that got us out of trouble, dodging our plane into the darkening clouds.

Back at base we found our plane was full of machine-gun holes. The mechanics discovered a fault in my oxygen supply too – that explained my hallucinations!

THE COMMANDER OF THE AMERICAN TROOPS WAS ASKED TO SURRENDER BY THE GERMANS - THIS WAS HIS FAMOUS REPLY...

NUTS!

THE GROUND CREWS WORKED HARD CLEARING THE RUNWAYS AND REPAIRING DAMAGED AIRCRAFT.

THE CONTROL TOWER MADE SURE WE ALL TOOK OFF AND LANDED SAFELY.

BATTLE OF THE BULGE

Snow choked the airfield that winter. That's when the Germans made a surprise counter-attack that came to be called "The Battle of the Bulge". They pushed forward and encircled many allied troops. But the Americans held out against the odds.

We did all we could to help the brave Yanks. But my war was about to come to a sudden end...

FILE COPY

TOTAL TIME ......

THIRTEENTH OP

We were flying through heavy 'boxed' flak, raiding Tiger tank supply depots when it happened. I remember us making the bombing run and hearing Com say, "BOMB DOORS OPEN. LEFT, LEFT. STEADY, STEADY... BOMBS GONE!" Then a shell burst close by...

Chunks of shrapnel punched through the aircraft. Bill's windscreen shattered. Filthy smoke rushed in and then something hit me in the face. It was like being kicked by an elephant! I blacked out.

I heard later that Bill had wrestled the plane back under control before checking everybody was OK on the intercom. When I didn't reply he sent Paddy to find me...

RAF HOSPITAL, 1945

ack at the airbase I was rushed away in an RAF
mbulance. When I woke up again it was Christmas
Day. The doc came and showed me my broken oxygen
mask. It had taken the full force of the impact.
I'd smashed my jaw – but I could have lost my head.

When my wounds had healed the
commanding officer must have
thought I'd done enough, because
he didn't send me back. He posted
me to a desk job in England
instead. And that's where I met
Muriel Jones...

> YOU'RE A LUCKY LAD!

THEY HAD TO OPERATE TO REMOVE THE
SHRAPNEL, BUT I WAS LUCKY TO BE ALIVE.

The war ended six months
later. I was a lucky boy. My war
ended with peace and love – and
that's how all war should end.

MURIEL JONES WAS A WAAF WIRELESS OPERATOR.
IT WAS LOVE AT FIRST SIGHT – BUT THAT'S
ANOTHER STORY!

TELEPHONE 4054
Headmaster : C. D. Manning.

Charlie Manning and Muriel Jones got married and they had four kids – including me! Dad gave away his flying jacket to a pal who had a motorbike; mum gave her uniform to a jumble sale. But like millions of other people, they kept their stories safe to pass on to us. How can we forget stories like that?

Mick

GLOSSARY

2ND TAF – The 2nd Tactical Air Force was made up of many fighter and bomber squadrons. After D-Day in 1944, 2nd TAF became the daylight air support for the Allied troops. Nazi leaders later admitted the 2nd TAF were crucial in their defeat.

AIRGUNNER – machine-gunners who defended the bombers against fighters.

ALLIES – countries fighting on the same side. Britain's allies included Australia, New Zealand, America, Canada and Russia. Germany's allies included Italy and Japan.

ANTI-AIRCRAFT GUNS – fired explosive shells set to burst at bomber height, scattering chunks of red-hot shrapnel across the sky that could smash a bomber to pieces, or set it on fire.

B25 MITCHELL – American-made bombers, popular with the crews that flew them.

BARRAGE BALLOON – carried thick cables into the sky to deter low-flying bombers.

BATTLE OF THE BULGE – a clever counter-attack by the Germans that took the allies by surprise in December 1944.

BILL, COM, CHARLIE AND PADDY – all survived the war. Bill went on to be a senior pilot for Air New Zealand and Charlie became a headmaster in Keighley, Yorkshire.

BOMBERS – planes that drop bombs on enemy targets.

BOY'S OWN COMIC – British comic of the 1940s filled with unrealistic, romanticised stories about war.

BRIEFING/DEBRIEFING – information about weather, dangers and targets given to, or brought back by, air crews before and after an operation.

BRYLCREEM – an oily hair cream fashionable at the time.

CHOCOLATE – RAF bomber crews got sandwiches, chocolate, malted milk tablets, and a hot drink to take on the long bombing raids.

CHURCHILL – Winston Churchill was the British Prime Minister during the war. He was a great leader in those dark days.

CIVIL DEFENCE – trained volunteers who helped people during the massive bombing raids on British towns by the Luftwaffe.

D-DAY – in June 1944, despite heavy casualties, the allied troops landed on French beaches and fought their way inland. The liberation of Europe had begun.

DITCHING DRILL – many planes were lost over the sea. It was important to learn how to survive in the water.

DUNKIRK – a seaside town in France where in 1940, despite merciless attacks from the advancing Germans, thousands of retreating British and French troops were rescued by ships and small boats.

FIGHTERS – planes that attack the enemy with guns or rockets.

FLAK – the name given to the smoky explosions of anti-aircraft guns.

GROUND CREW – included fitters, mechanics and engineers. They were essential to keep the squadron flying.

HALLUCINATION – seeing or hearing something that is not really there.

INTERCOM – the crew could talk to each other on the intercom.

LUFTWAFFE – the German air force. Its planes were some of the best in the world.

MELSBROEK – one of many European airbases taken over by the allies as the Germans retreated. Squadrons included 180, 98 and 320.

MESSERSCHMITT – (Mes-ser-sshmitt) one of the most deadly German fighters of the war.

NAAFI – short for Navy, Army, Air Force Institution. It served hot drinks and snacks to troops.

NAVIGATOR – read maps, plotted the route and was in charge of dropping the bombs.

NAZIS – a political party led by Adolf Hitler. They came to power in Germany in the 1930s by encouraging racism and patriotism and promising jobs and prosperity. They created a huge German army, invading many European countries. They arrested and murdered Jewish people, gypsies and anyone who disagreed with them. Millions of men, women and children were gassed or shot in special death camps. Some Germans opposed the Nazis but many kept silent through fear of Hitler's terrible secret police – the Gestapo.

OPERATIONAL TRAINING UNITS – where RAF recruits were given combat training.

PATRIOTISM – pride in your country.

PLEXIGLAS – a sort of plastic used instea of glass.

RAF – The Royal Air Force used fighters l Spitfires and Hurricanes for attack and defence. Despite huge air crew casualties RAF Bomber Command attacked enemy targets, mostly by night, using bombers like the Wellington, Halifax and Lancaster.

RACISM – the idea that one race, or colour, of people is better than another.

RATION COUPONS – German U-boats sunk a lot of the ships bringing supplies to Britain. Food and clothing had to be rationed to make sure everyone got a share.

SHRAPNEL – deadly chunks of sharp metal from an exploding bomb or shell.

SQUADRON – an organised group of fighters or bombers.

SQUARE-BASHING – basic training, including marching and saluting.

OBSERVER'S AND AIR GUNNER'S FLYING LOG BOOK

TAIL-END CHARLIE – the airgunner in the tail-turret had a very low chance of survival. In some cases a life expectancy of only 3 missions.

TRACER – every sixth machine gun bullet might be a tracer – a glowing coloured bullet that shows the direction of fire.

WAAF – Women's Auxiliary Air Force.

WAIST-GUNS – some bombers had gunners' windows on both sides to protect the sides of the plane.

WELLINGTON – a British-made bomber that was used throughout the war.

WIRELESS OPERATOR – sent and received messages and often doubled as an airgunner.

WORLD WAR TWO – began in 1939 when the German leader, Adolf Hitler, ordered his army to invade Poland. Other countries, including Norway, Holland, Belgium, Denmark, Greece and France, quickly fell to the Germans and their allies, Italy. Britain fought back with help from Australia, India, Canada and New Zealand. During the Battle of Britain, the RAF successfully defeated the German Luftwaffe, forcing the Germans to call off a planned invasion of Britain. The RAF also raided Germany, and allied soldiers fought in the Middle East and Asia. On 22nd June 1941 Germany invaded Russia. Their allies, Japan, bombed the American Navy at Pearl Harbour on the 7th December 1941. This brought the huge armies of America and Russia into the war. In 1944, as the Russians fought the Germans on the Eastern front, America and Britain invaded France. After terrible fighting Germany finally surrendered in 1945. A few months later Japan surrendered after America dropped the first atomic bombs.

YANKS – a nickname for Americans.